SYMPHONIES, SHAMROCKS AND SONGS

POEMS

Marian Grady McNeely

SYMPHONIES, SHAMROCKS AND SONGS

Poems

by Marian Grady McNeely

Bristol Banner Books
Publishing
since 1877

Typesetting by M & M Typeset, Middlebury, IN   46540.

Library of Congress Catalog Card Number

91-077716

ISBN 1-879183-15-3

I dedicate this book to my husband, Walter, to my children, my "in-law" children and my beautiful grand-children who are all very much a part of these verses.

Dear
Maureen and
Larry -
Hope you enjoy these
verses -
Love -
Maureen

TABLE OF CONTENTS

LIGHT VERSE

VERSES FOR CHILDREN

SHAMROCKS

HAIKU
Japanese Poetry Form

TANKA
Japanese Poetry Form

iv   Marian Grady McNeely

OLD WARRIORS ON THE WHARF

LOVE'S MELODY

It seems, my dearest one, that I've been loving you forever
For all the sweet and thoughtful things you do
For all the times you held my hand, and smiled and reassured me
But most of all, dear, just for being you

We've walked together, counted stars, and watched the morning sunrise
We've seen the springtime flowers breaking through
And each time that we watched the sunlight sparkle on the water
I thanked God I was watching it with you

Down through the years our love has grown, in fair and stormy weather
Our joys have multiplied one hundredfold
And we have kept our vows, and worked the bad times out together
While weaving memories of purest gold

Through many precious moments that we've shared with one another
I've asked our God to keep us in his care
For every day will always have a very special meaning
Just knowing, my dear one, that you are there

SWEET SYNCHRONICITY

Our lives are a lovely melody
As hand in hand we go
Our heartbeats are the rhythm
You're the fiddle, I'm the bow

A needlepointed masterpiece
On which these words are said
"Our home is where the heart is"
You're the needle. I'm the thread

We tell a sweet love story
Of memories 'way back when'
A book bound by contentment
You're the paper, I'm the pen

Our marriage is a gourmet feast
On which our dreams are fed
Seasoned with our years together
You're the butter, I'm the bread

And in our brilliant galaxy
A light shines from afar
And twinkles with our happiness
You're the sun and I'm your star

TO MOTHER

You've always been a special friend
In your reassuring way
With soothing words of comfort
That only you could say

When things would get a little tough
You were always there
No matter what the reason
We knew that you would care

Our memories of childhood days
Are laced with visions true
Of parties and of playgrounds
Yet quiet moments, too

You helped us with our homework
And helped lace up our skates
And worried some and prayed some more
When we were late from dates

As each new little family grew
We'd good days, bad ones, too
But when a problem would arise
Your prayers would see us through

And when our fates would dictate
That we would have to roam
The joy was in returning
To you, our heart, our home

For God gave us a treasure
Far greater than we knew
When He said, "Child, behold your mother!"
Then He gave us you

A MAN CALLED PAT

He would sit there in the corner with his fiddle to his chin
And the room was filled with music at his touch
All cares and woes were put aside whenever he was playing
And you knew he loved his music very much

With his ever-present smile while his foot tapped out the rhythm
The bow would fairly fly across the strings
And we girls would step lively to a lovely Irish hornpipe
To add to pleasures only music brings

And how he loved his homeland, that lovely little isle
With the shamrock and the heather blooming fair
And he'd play a little softer and a tear would dim his eye
When he thought of the dear mother he left there

We'd thrill to wondrous stories he would tell us of the sea
When the winds were raging on the restless foam
How, through the lashing rain and crashing waters all around him,
He would turn his craft and bring it safely home

We would hear about the lighthouse on Clare Island's rugged cliffs
And how he'd guide the boats that might pass by
So now we sometimes wonder is he helping guide lost souls
To Heaven from that lighthouse in the sky

And yet, he loved America, the land that he had chosen
Worked hard to give us all a happy home
And with his music and his love left many happy memories
We'll not forget wherever we may roam

Now sometimes in the day, I close my eyes and think of Heaven
All gold and white with twinkling stars so bright
And I see him in the corner with his fiddle to his chin
And I find myself just smiling at the sight

There an Irish jig is playing, all his friends are dancing 'round
And Heav'n is even sweeter for the sound
Then I look up at the Throne and there I see a sandal tapping
And a gentle Lord is smiling down upon . . .

MY DAD, A MAN CALLED PAT

MY CHILDREN IN PROSE AND POETRY

Where are my children of yesteryear
My little ones laughing at play
Gone from my grasp, but in memory
So close as though it were today

    There's sweet little Kathie, hardly bigger than
    the baton she carried, proudly marching down the
    street after the high school band, wanting so
    much to be a part of it . . .

Yes, where are the children that needed me so
Where did they go? Where did they go?

    And precious little Geri, someone's older sister
    in age and responsibility by the time she was two,
    and I want to reach out and give her one of the hugs
    she missed when the younger babies all got theirs . . .

Where are the small ones that played in the pool
And worried me so when they came late from school

    And there's Tom, dear little Tommy, who, though
    obviously nervous on the first day of school, but
    not wanting to show it, walked bravely into
    kindergarten not even turning to wave good-bye . . .

When did they leave me, each dear little one
My four lovely daughters, my one precious son

    And lovely little Mimi, only five, who at school
    introduced the kindergarten program, spoke on the
    P.A., but at home, always checking to make sure
    Mom was still there . . .

When did they vanish, all these children fair
It seemed that a moment ago, they were there

> And darling little Theresie, who, barely as high as
> the step itself, ruled the neighborhood from our front
> porch, charming even the grown-ups . . .

And yet, as I ponder, there's a knock on the door
And as they walk in, I need question no more
I know where they are, all these children of mine
They're now young adults, and they're doing just fine
And I smile to myself as I look at this crowd
And I say, "I'm their Mom, and am I ever proud!!!"

ON FIRST SEEING MY GRANDSON

I hold you
Your delicate sweet features so familiar
Yet never seen before
The warmth of your soft body reassures me
Of the miracle of life
And, oh, what wondrous gifts that I would give you
Not just material things
But precious gifts beyond the realm of man
That you would know the beauty of the first spring rose
The soft, moist rain upon your face
Enjoy the vastness of the bright blue sky
And tan your strong young body in the sun
But more than this, that you would know serenity
In a world torn by bitterness and strife
That you will set your goal in life, then follow it
And not be stirred by those who would deter you
Then may you have the courage of conviction
And stand by your beliefs
No matter who or what would have it otherwise
For, Little One, the world is yours from this day on
Not yet to mold, for you are but a babe
But just to hold - and as you grow, to fashion
Until the day that you emerge, a man!

WORDS THAT MAKE A GRANDDAUGHTER

Pretty and precious
and pastel pink

Serious, sentimental
And so, so sweet

Whispering, winsome, wise
And quite wonderful

Dainty and darling
And delicate

Clutching her dolly
And her daddy's hand

And her Grandma's heart!

GRANDMA

There are jewels rare from India, the purest
   Chinese silks
And diamonds cut to catch each brilliant light
There are pearls rubbed and polished from the
   oysters of the sea
And twinkling stars that light the velvet night

But they all pale by comparison when shining toddler's
   eyes
Look into mine and with a baby lisp
Wraps chubby arms around me and says "Grandma, I love you!"
Then on my cheek, he plants a big moist kiss!

LADY OF LIBERTY

Lady of Liberty, your torch held on high
Beloved of all your fair children around you
Beloved of all who have looked to your shores
The blue skies of freedom will ever surround you

You stand like an angel at hard journey's end
And gather the masses that yearn to breathe free
The tired, the poor, the lost and the homeless
Who have braved wind and weather for sweet liberty

Our voices are raised now in love and affection
To honor this country so proudly we hail
May our flag always wave in the fair winds of freedom
Oh, Lady of Love, may your cause never fail

MY PRAYER

I am Your creation
Made in Your Image and Likeness
Receiver of Your countless gifts
A chalice filled with Your forgiveness
Born of Your love and caring
Bestowed with Your many graces
Touched by Your precious Hands

And knowing this, I raise my eyes to Heaven
Remembering these gifts and boundless love
To say this humble prayer of sweet thanksgiving
For all abundant blessings from above

But, when I see the honor and the majesty
My God, Almighty to a finite me
And dwell upon divine and awesome mysteries
The glory of a Godhead, One in Three

I have no voice, no sound, no way to pray
And in my human-ness, can only say

MY LORD AND MY GOD!

FAITH

I have to believe someone hears me
In my moments of darkest despair
When I pray to a God all forgiving
I have to believe that He's there

I have to believe Heaven awaits me
As I trudge through mundane chores so trite
I have to believe there's a sunrise
At the end of a long troubled night

And when Earth's dreary passage is over
And my last tired step I have trod
I have to believe I'll be nestled
Content - in the arms of my God

FRAGILE

Life is a gift from our Father in Heaven
Like a rose blooming brightly in a garden so fair
It needs to be tended and nurtured and cared for
Life is so fragile - handle with prayer

A prayer of thanksgiving to God, our creator
To show that we're grateful for His tender care
To show with each heartbeat how much we do love Him
Yes, life is so precious, please handle with prayer

CELESTIAL CONNECTION

If I had a hot line to Heaven
I'd pick up the 'phone and I'd say
"Sweet Jesus, I just called to thank you
For the sun shining brightly today,

For the birds with their colorful plumage
As they dart, back and forth, tree to tree
And, pledging their love to each other,
Fill the air with their sweet harmony."

I'd say, "Thank you dear God for my family
And dear friends that we meet every day
For the pleasures of music and laughter
And the sounds of the children at play."

Then I'd ask my dear Lord just to bless me
And walk with me when I despair
To carry me when steps are heavy
And keep us all in His sweet care

Yet now as I think on it further
We're all blest with treasure so rare
For we <u>DO</u> have a hot line to Heaven
Each time that we utter a prayer!

MARY'S CROWN

"Hail Mary, full of grace," recite the little voices
Innocence and love on bended knee
And, one by one, the beads are said amid the flickering candles
Sweet roses formed in perfect harmony

While, in the heavens above, our Blessed Lady sits in splendor
And while the children pray, her eyes look down
She smiles a lovely smile, then tilts her head a little forward
To accept their loving gift, her rosary crown

PRAYER FOR THE CHILDREN LOST

Dear Lady, Queen of Heaven, bless the children
All those in far-off lands and here at home
So many are alone, be their protector
And guide them through the hostile lands they roam

Be with them as they struggle for survival
Through endless days of hunger and of pain
And give their mothers hope in human kindness
That their babies might be well and strong again

For Mary, of all Mothers, you have suffered, too
You lost your son, then later, watched Him die
So bless these little fragile lives with torment crossed
Lest they, in hopelessness, be left to cry

Please, Mary, in your love, reach out and touch them all
Yes, let these children feel your healing care
And Mother of all mothers, touch each tiny heart
Bring warmth and love to children everywhere

THE WAITING GAME

The baby waits
Big tears roll down his chubby, dimpled cheeks
He's hungry and he is waiting to be fed
And so begins a series of life's waitings
As the baby frets and waits

Susan smiles
Jim promised he would pick her up at 8
Her young heart beats in sweet anticipation
Tonight, together, they will choose the ring
And Susan waits

Mother waits anxiously
The hour is late, the children not yet home
With furrowed brow, she paces back and forth
Why does each hour seem a whole year long
When you are waiting

And Grandad waits
An old friend from a war so long ago
Has written that he's coming for a visit
Memories come flooding back -- he smiles
Then sets to wait

Great Grandmum rocks and waits
Her time-worn fingers counting out the beads
Three generations follow in her footsteps
Tired now, she wants her wait to end
She nods, then hears a gentle, sweet voice say
"Dear One, you've waited patiently so long
This day you'll come to be with me in Paradise"
Her waiting ends!

A child stirs
Within the womb, he's waiting to be born . . .

GOOD FRIDAY

The Cross stands stark against the darkened, angry sky
　　Beneath the wood, low, saddened moans are heard
As life ebbs slowly from the Nazarean
　　A death by crucifixion for the "Word"

A crown of thorns is pressed against His aching head
　　While tears of sorrow ridge the youthful face
And prayers of sweet forgiveness leave His quiet lips
　　For those He loved now fallen from His grace

A grieving moan is heard throughout the blackened sky
　　As Mary lifts her eyes up to the cross
And sees her own beloved son with arms outstretched
　　Then feels an anguished, devastating loss

The women sob, the sun slips down behind the clouds
　　While Jesus cries in terrible despair
"My God, My Father, why have you forsaken me?"
　　Then bows His head again in quiet prayer

This day, forever, will go down in infamy
　　A day that man disgraced his very soul
And sold his God for thirty silver pieces
　　To a world so uncaring, cruel and cold

ACCEPTANCE

The x-rays confirm it
A tumor bigger than life
And maybe deadly

I wring my hands and try to stay calm
While a knot swells in my abdomen
That all but consumes me

This cannot be
Things like this don't happen
To people like me
Yet, slowly, realization settles in
Like a cold winter's fog

I am not exempt
I have no shield, no armor
Against this thing

Tears don't help
They only cause a hurtful brow
And blotches

All are supportive
But this battle is mine alone to wage

Attitude, they say, will help recovery
But when the only attitude is fear
How does one cope

Chemotherapy, the dreaded word
And yet, the only hope
And so we deal with it

Quietly, I accept my fate
And know, now, that I must pray
As I have never prayed before

That I must fight
And I must win
And with God's help, I WILL

A YOUNG WIDOW'S LAMENT

I'm crying because you've left me and you're gone
Your warm young body taken from my arms
And, in my grief, I find a new emotion
I'm angry, oh so very angry, too
I never thought that you would just abandon me
Expect me to go on day after day
You left me here with needs, with human needs
Emotional and spiritual and physical
All tightly meshed in your young life like fine crochet
And now those needs hang loosely like broken threads
Never to be picked up and made whole again
Never to be satisfied at all
My heart cries out in terrible despair
And as I listen to the echoes of my silent screams,
I realize that you are gone forever
And I must find my way out of the darkness
- Alone -

WHEN GRANDMA DIED

The young nurse walked into the room
   As evening sun was falling
And found the lifeless body on the bed
She listened at the chest for heartbeat,
   at the wrist for pulse
Then gently pulled the sheet above her head

But no one heard the angel's song
   that swelled in celebration
And filled the halls with glorious melody
Nor saw sweet Mary robed in white come
   walking on a ray of light
And say, "Come, you will meet my Son with me!"

Then Cherubim and Seraphim rejoiced in
   wondrous splendor
And paved the way to Heaven with jewels rare
The trumpets heralded their coming while the
   harps with joyous strumming
Accompanied our Grandma to His chair

Yet in that darkened room that day
They only said, "She's passed away."

Her own remembered and they cried
But Heav'n rejoiced when Grandma died

MY LEGACY

What will I leave when I am gone
What have I ever done
What feats have I accomplished
Or battles have I won

And when my name is mentioned
Will anyone recall
Will anyone remember
That I was here at all

Will my life have made a difference
To any other life
Have I calmed some troubled waters
In a world torn by strife

Can I say that my presence here
On this unsettled earth
Brought joy to just one person
If but a moment's worth

I ponder in these golden years
They're fraught with fears, I find
And worry of the legacy
That I will leave behind

And then I see my family
Four daughters and a son
A sweet bouquet of blessings
I count them, every one

Yes, they will be my legacy
When I am called above
I leave behind my children
My legacy of love

AT JOURNEY'S END

I know
That where I'll go
Will be a better place

But I will miss
Each tender kiss
Each loving gentle face

The precious touch
I love so much
The hug when day is done

The hands I held
Sweet joys I felt
Brought happiness and fun

The plans we made
And dreams that fade
Were all a part of life

Love's moments seen
The bond between
A husband and a wife

Yet cry no tears
But bless the years
The good ones and the bad

And thank our God
For steps I've trod
Each blessed joy I've had

So when at last
When years have passed
You sit in memory

Clasp hands and smile
And for a while
Please just remember me

SALUTE TO AMERICA

A   is for America, our land of liberty

M   is for the mighty men who died to keep her free

E   is for each ethnic group who came from lands oppressed
to build a strong new nation and fulfill their valiant quest

R   for rights to liberty and life and happiness

I   ideals, may they be high, no matter what the stress

C   courageous children from each and every state
working hand in hand as one to keep their country great

A   is for allegiance to our nation young and brave
as we salute Old Glory; long may she proudly wave

America, our prayers for you will echo shore to shore
for courage and for brotherhood and peace forever more

AMERICA'S PRIDE

The breezes sway the restless poppies on his grave
He went to war a boy, but died a man
His name forever etched on history's tabloids
Names written in their blood since time began

It matters not which side for which these brave men fought
It matters less the colors that they bore
But only that each soldier gave his fine young life
To honor the proud uniform he wore

So let no one forget this selfless sacrifice
Let's strive to right a devestating wrong
Of man's unthinking inhumanity to man
And place our values back where they belong

Let's count the lives of each man strong and young and brave
As precious gems among our treasures rare
Remembering the hateful violations
That took those lives and finally laid them there

I place a single rose upon his lonely grave
And poets before me have said it best
Oh God, these brave young men have given all they had
So, in Your love, give them eternal rest

LIGHT VERSE

MY MID-LIFE CRISIS (or lack of one)

They told me in mid-life, the kids would be gone
And Hubby would make his own way
And I would be lonely, despondent and wan
'Cause nobody needs me today

I sit with my coffee and ponder these things
When the phone starts to ring off the wall
It's my daughter, her husband has taken the car
And she needs a quick ride to the mall

And, oh, by the way, when the boys come from school
Could they stay here with me for a while
And did I remember they'll be here for dinner?
She hangs up the phone and I smile

The teenage brigade hops off the school bus
And boisterously bursts through the door
"Hey, Mom, are my jeans dry - and what's there to eat?
Don't you buy nothin' good any more??

We practice tonight, Mom, I hope you've remembered
And I have to be there by eight!"
"Oh, good, on the way, Mom, drop us at the party
We surely don't want to be late!"

Oh oh, here comes Grandma now hot at my heels
Again, she has mixed up her pills
"Now, dear, you get busy and sort these all out
I need the right ones for my ills."

"Hi, hon, what's for dinner?" Oh, Hubby is home
"Boy - have I had a bad day
I just want to rest, can you pick up the kids
From their games?", then he ambles away

Now, when people bring up "mid-life crisis" to me
As I'm rushing without and within
I say, "Hey, forget it, I just don't have time
I've tried, but I can't fit it in!!!"

SPRING'S SONG

A magic fairy gowned in white
Emerged from winter snow
And raised her wand up to the light
It's magic, too, you know

And when it glistened in the sun
She gently touched the earth
And all the snow began to melt
To hasten spring's rebirth

The tiny little crocus
And daffodils of gold
Began to peek up through the ground
And tulips bright and bold

Were breaking through in clusters
Each one a gay bouquet
With colors, purple, red, and gold
To brighten each new day

And soon the air was filled with song
And robins in the trees
Were heralding a brand new spring
On every gentle breeze

A FEW WORDS ABOUT SPRING

It's spring and the season of sunshine and birds
It's spring and the time to write poetic words
Words like roses and blossoms and "light airy breezes"
And lovers and kisses and hugs and "tight squeezes"
And who can forget words like romantic moons
Or fleecy clouds, sunny skies, small tight cocoons
And we thrill to the sound of the cute honeybees
And the rain softly falling on fragrant peach trees
But there are three words of spring, not poetic at all
In fact, just to think of them makes my flesh crawl
They actually seem without reason or rhyme
To this poet! What are they?????

"IT'S HOUSECLEANING TIME!"

MY ROBIN

I keep my happy vigil at my window
As soon as tiny daffodils appear
And gentle zephyrs warm the coldest winter heart
For then I know my special friend is near

Each year we plan an early springtime rendezvous
And soon I hear the song I knew would come
He sings "I'm back again, were you expecting me?"
I say "Oh yes, my friend - and welcome home"

SWEET SOUNDS OF SUMMER

I stand in my garden and listen
To the sweet music that fills the air
To the buzzing of bees
As they move through the trees
And the rustling of lilacs so fair

Then I thrill to the song of the robin
As he calls to his mate lovingly
And the flutter of wings
As the bright goldfinch sings
While he's flitting from feeder to tree

The crows caw and scold at each other
While the cardinal sings his royal song
And the warm summer breeze
Through the whispering trees
Plays a soft melody all day long

So I smile as I stand in my garden
And enjoy all the melodies fair
For my day is complete
with the music so sweet
And I'm happy to just linger there

SOME THOUGHTS ABOUT AUTUMN

The smell of crisp leaves burning fill the air
And yet, late summer roses sweetly bloom
Vases filled with bright orange bittersweet
Decorate each cozy family room

It seems, now, that the whole world turns to gold
With fiery, scarlet reds of deepest hue
Deftly splashed against a bright blue sky
To give a striking panoramic view

It's autumn - and the loveliest time of year
When summer's not yet gone, nor winter come
And roses, daisies and primroses, too
Bloom brightly alongside each autumn "mum"

So now, before these vivid colors go
And fade into a bed of winter gray
Let's stop and take a moment to enjoy
This precious gift, a lovely autumn day!

TWO FACES OF WINTER

"When winter comes, can spring be far behind?"
We've oft-times heard this old cliche, it's true
But winter isn't really all that bad!
Let's see it from a different point of view

Let's watch the sunlight glisten on the snow
Like a thousand glimmering diamonds set in white
And see majestic evergreens bow low
To the cool and moonlit stillness of the night

Let's thrill to children's voices clear and bright
As they build snowmen reaching to the sky
Or watch them making "angels" in the snow
Or trying to catch snowflakes as they fly

And look! Amid the sledtracks on the hill
A little rabbit dashes to and fro
Then stops short, darting glances left and right
As though he's just not sure which way to go

Yes, winter weaves her magic for us all
The icicles that glisten in the sun
Snow-capped trees and rippled frozen streams
And a roaring, crackling fire when day is done

But when things like bitter winds and icy walks
And virus colds and bad falls come to mind
We just can't blame the wistful souls who say
"When winter comes, can spring be far behind?"

THE LAST LAUGH

Our cars are all stuck in rock-hard icy drifts
And the snow is piled high on the drive
While the wind tears our hats from our heads as it
blows
And we just don't know how we'll survive
And that old winter moon - he just lies on
his back and he laughs

Our cheeks are all chapped and our fingers are
stiff
Our backs ache from sweeping and shovelling
And icicles form on our brows and eyelashes
As through snow and wet slush we are struggling
Yet that old winter moon - he just lies on his
back and he laughs

We're all sick with colds and each new strain of
virus
Our ears are plugged up and we cough
The water's all frozen but our noses are running
And we've no way of turning them off
But that old winter moon - he just lies on his
back and he laughs

Now, someday, that old winter moon will find out
That a spring moon now floats in his place
And the King of all Nature maneuvers the stars
And wipes that big smirk from the winter moon's
face
Then that old winter moon, to a different tune, will
be gone
        AND WE'LL LAUGH!!

PRIORITIES

I say today it will be better
As I wake up to the sun
I'll really get my act together
Really going to get things done

I shower, dress and make the beds
Then go downstairs to start the day
The phone rings - Oh, it's Eleanor
Well, let's see what she has to say

"I don't believe it, Eleanor
She couldn't have - No! Really?
They did! You didn't! Are you sure?
Oh, Eleanor - you're kidding me!"

And so it goes until two hours
Have bit the dust (it's there to bite)
Now I must rush all afternoon
To be all finished by tonight

I start to dust - oh, there's that book
I started, but then put aside
I wonder if Rhett hated Scarlett
When he found out that she lied

Hours later I close the book
But then I notice to my sorrow
My household chores are all still there
Oh well, I'll do them all tomorrow

THE GAL NEXT DOOR

She's attractive, she's pretty
At parties she's witty
She's man's perfect mate

Her home is a showplace
She never goes no-place
Without looking great

She knows how to dress
And I've got to confess
Her hair's the real color

At party's late hour
She has "sparkle" power
While I just get duller

She serves on committees
From suburbs to cities
A real super gal

And yet anywhere
When she's needed, she's there
She's everyone's "pal"

So "Who needs her", I say
As I plod through each day
"Who indeed - to what end?"

Then with feelings true blue
I admit that I do
She's my dearest best friend!

AGE HAS IT'S PRIVILEGES

They say, don't grow old gracefully,
   don't let the wrinkles show!
Nor let the 'crow's feet' dance upon your face
Keep jumping up and down to change the cellulose
   to firm
And though your feet hurt, always walk with grace

Don't let your eye-lids overlap, no bags below
   those eyes
Allow no pouches on your satin cheeks
And walk around with hunger pangs until you want
   to cry
To lose a pound or two though it takes weeks

Well, I say, just forget it - don't quote that stuff
   to me
"Age has its privilege" so they've always said
And I can walk as gracefully with a milk shake in
   my hand
As balancing a book upon my head

I do use 'creams' - they're butter creams dipped in
   chocolate sweet
My exercise is running to the store
For when I dip my hand into an almost empty box
It's imperative to run out and get more!

So with T. V. and 'bon-bons' near, I curl up on my
   couch
And munch some goodies to my heart's delight
And when old age comes riding hard upon my wrinkled
   heels
I'll just give in - it's too much work to fight!

THE WAY WE WERE

We were here before T. V.
Before the 'pill' and 'contact lenses'
We hadn't heard of credit cards
And no one drove 'Mercedes Benzes'

'Grass' was mowed, we drank our 'coke'
A 'pot' cooked up the evening meal
McDonald's had yet to make their 'first'
And an "Apple" was something you could peel

We loved our penny candy treats
The 'free' stick on an ice cream bar
And a 'compact' was a powder case
And not a snappy little car

We hit the scene before computers
'Soft wear' then, was lingerie
A 'chip' was just a piece of wood
And when you were happy, you were gay

Frozen foods weren't heard of yet
Ball point pens nor panty hose
Penicillin was still just 'mold'
And no one knew of 'drip-dry' clothes

Back then, we thought that all 'fast foods'
Were meals that Mom cooked during Lent
A 'clothes-dryer' was a line out back
And a stick of gum cost just one cent

'Rock Music' was a lullabye
Cuddled warm in Grandma's chair
"Aids" helped out the teachers then
And no one breathed 'conditioned air'

Those were our times, the best, the worst
Our parents, then, were M'am and Sir
And yet, our lives were simpler then
Those magic years, the way we were

VERSES
FOR
CHILDREN

A GIFT OF WARMTH - A GIFT OF LOVE

A little lamb was lying in the stable
The night was cold, the sky so very bright
While all his friends were playing on the hillside
As stars lit up the beauty of the night

A twisted leg had left the small lamb helpless
He couldn't frolic with his friends at all
And he was feeling sad and, oh, so lonely
Then fell asleep against the stable wall

When, all at once, he wakened to a haunting sound
As Mary sang a soft, sweet lullaby
And Baby Jesus shivered in the cold night air
While a brilliant star lit up the winter sky

Then Joseph came and gently took the tiny lamb
And laid him near the infant on the straw
"His fur will help to keep our little baby warm,"
Said Joseph - and the lamb was filled with awe

For songs of angels swelled above the stable now
And "Peace to Men" called shepherds in the field
And when the lamb stood up, his little legs were strong
He looked down and his twisted leg was healed

The baby smiled and raised a tiny, dimpled hand
To stroke the lamb, while angels from above
Spread joyous tidings to the people everywhere
Of a child born to fill the world with love

MY LITTLE BROTHER

Mommy brought a present home
I'd rather have another
She didn't bring a game or doll
She brought a baby brother

And ever since they brought him home
They hardly ever see me
They're spending all their time with him
Especially when he's "screamy"

And when he makes those gurgling sounds
Mom and Dad just smile
And I feel kind of lonely
If only for a while

But just today he smiled at me
And I held his tiny hand
And tickled him, he laughed with glee
And really, it was grand

Daddy said I shouldn't feel
That they don't love me too
Or think I'm just as special
Because they really do

Mommy says when Baby sleeps
The angels sing above him
Now when I see him in his crib
I guess I really love him

SWEET INNOCENCE

A dear little child at play one day
Said, "Mommy, who takes the moon away
And puts the sun back in the sky
And when it rains, does the sandman cry

Why is the robin's song so sweet
And where did the centipede get all those feet
Who colors the wings on a butterfly
And what makes an airplane fly so high?"

Then Mommy sat and thought for a while
And she looked at her child with a loving smile
Then said, "My dear one, as angels have wings
And the heavens have stars, God does _all_ things!"

KRISTIN KITTEN'S NEW HOME

Little Kristin Kitten walked slowly down the lane
She wondered if she'd ever find a happy home again
Her master, Mr. Twilliby, had taken a new wife
There was no place for little cats or kittens in her life

Kristin thought about this morning, while playing on the floor
She looked and saw the Mistress pointing firmly toward the door
"All right, Kristin Kitten, now you must go away
We want no cats around this house, not now or any day"

Her heart was almost breaking as she walked along the lane
She really didn't know how she would ever bear the pain
She looked to see a bright side, she did, she really tried
But finally she just gave in and sat right down and cried

A little boy was passing by and saw poor little Kris
He picked her up and brought her home to Mom who said, "What's this?"
"It's just a little kitty, Mom, may we keep her here with us?
I promise I'll take care of her and she won't make a fuss"

And Mom just smiled and said, "Of course! We'll make a bed for her"
And then they laid the kitten down and she began to purr
"Oh!" Kristin thought, "How wonderful, how lucky I have been"
For little Kristin Kitten found a happy home again

SOME "BEAR FACTS"

He comes from deep Australia, this furry little friend
To kangaroo and platypus, his greetings he might send
Some say that way "down under" is a strange place for a bear
But all little "KOALAS" seem very happy there

The "POLAR BEAR" with creamy fur is found where it is cold
He is quite good at swimming and diving, we are told
The baby seals and walruses must move with utmost care
They wouldn't want to be a "meal" for a "POLAR BEAR"

The "BLACK BEAR OF AMERICA" is a friendly bear
If you have been to Yellowstone, you may have seen him there
These bears walk up to travelers and beg for food and sweets
They are so tame they sit right down and do enjoy their treats

The bear we see in the circus is "EUROPE'S BIG BROWN BEAR"
These bears are trained to dance and to perform with tender care
Sometimes they seem quite human when appearing in a show
And almost seem to smile as they are moving to and fro

But there's one bear out of all the rest that's loved so very much
That little boys and little girls just love to hug and touch
And take to bed and cuddle warmly as they're lying there
And we all know who that one is - your own sweet "TEDDY BEAR"

BOOKS

I love to sit and read my books
They take me far away
I read about the places
I'd like to go someday

I read about the heroes
Of our nation, brave and true
Of hardships pioneers endured
And how they saw them through

My books tell me of astronauts
Who landed on the moon
Of traveling in space some day
Some say it might be soon

And with my books, I wander through
The ancient ruins of Rome
Through palaces and kingdoms grand
And then come safely home

For books are like an open door
And if you'll just step through
There's a world of wondrous things
Just waiting there for you

BRIGHT COLORS - BRIGHT DAYS

When I can use my brush and paints
I go to wondrous places
I fashion men with cloak and sword
And oriental faces
And southern belles with hoop skirts
And soldiers brave and tall
Yes, any country in the world
Is at my beck and call

So when the thunder starts to roll
And it begins to rain
I'll not be standing sadly looking
Through my window pane
For I'll be busy all day long
And you'll hear no complaint
The world is at my fingertips
Whenever I can paint!

PRINCE

His name was Prince, and he was known to children far and near
He was a prancing circus horse, a horse that knew no fear
From town to town he traveled, with the "Big Top" and its crew
And every child in every town knew Prince, he knew them too

His golden mane would fly as his hooves pounded on the ground
And "bareback riders" turned and twisted as he pranced around
And then, his noble head held high, Prince would take his bow
Oh how he longed for those good times, but things were different now

For Prince was old, could prance no more, his circus days were through
He longed to be with all his friends, the children that he knew
But oh alas, he stood alone in a field next to the tent
He felt so blue, his heart was sad, his once proud head was bent

Then one day, the circus man brought a blanket gold and red
"Prince, you'll give the children rides upon your back," he said
The horse trembled with excitement as he stood there tall and proud
And when the children saw him, they began to cry aloud,

"It's Prince, it's Prince, we've missed you Prince, so please don't go away
We want you Prince, we love you, and we hope you're going to stay!"
And he could hardly bear the pain of happiness inside
As little voices loud and clear cried, "Prince, just one more ride!"

And so it went, the whole day long, and Prince, his head held high,
Enjoying every step he took, each happy child's cry,
Said, "Look at me, it's wonderful, how lucky I have been!"
For Prince was with his little friends, the children, once again!

SHAMROCKS

HAPPINESS IS BEING IRISH

I love my Irishness
I love the little land with shamrock fair
Where strains of lilting music fill the air
And lovely Irish smiles are everywhere
Oh yes, I must confess
I love my Irishness

I love my Irishness
I love the way the mustic makes me feel
Each ballad sweet, each lively jig and reel
And laughing Irish eyes your heart to steal
I will admit, no less
I love my Irishness

I love my Irishness
I love to wear my 'green' on Paddy's day
And smile at passers-by and wink and say
"Top o' the mornin' on this special day!"
I truly must confess
I love my Irishness

I guess I'm feelin' so inspirish
Cause happiness is being Irish!

A PRAYER FOR IRELAND

We pray for you, Ireland, for peace in your valleys
For peace in your mountains, each river and glen
That God will protect you, dear land of our
    forebears
And join all your counties together again

That your own "Golden Rose", our dear Lady, will bless
    you
And beg of her Son, a true peace that will last
For your children to join hands across every ocean
And blot out the memories of a war-weary past

We will all pray together for the sweet blooming shamrock
For the heather that sways in the wind on the moor
That our God will reach out with His choicest of
    blessings
And make you one nation, one land as before

Yes, we pray for you, Ireland, for strength in your
    struggles
That God guide each hand with His powerful love
And bring all together in peace and in friendship
As He blesses your land with His grace from above

DRIVING DOWN THE LITTLE ROADS OF IRELAND

We start out on a beautiful day
With roses blooming along the way
And the sun smiling down on the shamrock green
Sure, a lovelier sight you have never seen
Than when driving down the little roads of Ireland

The scent of turf fire fills the air
While sheep are grazing here and there
The children wave as we go along
And delight us with each childlike song
While driving down the little roads of Ireland

Along the road, a grotto stands
Of Mary and in her praying hands
A rosary is enfolded there
And so we stop and say a prayer
While driving down the little roads of Ireland

At every turn, there's a friendly face
Willing to show us whatever place
We are looking for - as we ride along
While humming a bit of an Irish song
And driving down the little roads of Ireland

The furze in the field is golden bright
And the shadings of green, a breath-taking sight
The farmer waves his cap with a smile
And all stress is forgotten if just for a while
As we're driving down the little roads of Ireland

So, as we enjoy each different place
Each scenic view, each smiling face
I know for sure, at least for me
There is no place I would rather be
Than driving down the little roads of Ireland

WATCHING IRISH SKIES

I love to watch them
The skies over Ireland
Changing, ever changing skies

In morning mist
The mountain tops are lost
But moments later
Appear again through spreading sunlight
In a sky washed clean
With fine soft rain

Cool afternoon skies
Play shadow-dancing with the sun
As moving opaque clouds
Run along the hillside
Creating gauzy patterns
On daisy-spilled meadows
And "patch work quilt" fields

Rain clouds gathering
Are a threatening gray
And scurry faster and faster
Bringing with them the lashing rain
But again, within moments
The wind has chased the clouds away
And Father Sun
Takes his royal place
In the beautiful Irish sky

Sometimes, there is a melancholy sadness
In those skies
But mostly, a soothing calmness
And pleasant reassurance
In Nature's beauty
As we watch with pleasure
The ever changing skies
Over Ireland

A SONG OF CONNEMARA

Oh, how we love the song you sing, O lovely Connemara
The happy songs of children as they play among your flowers
Of bubbling brooks that dance along your blossom covered meadows
And little lambs that frolic on your mountainside and bowers

But in the stillness of your wild and bold majestic beauty
We hear another melody, the lonely saddened strain
Of mothers weeping for their sons; of young wives, for their husbands
Who, beaten by a raging sea, would ne'er return again

And high above your mountaintops, the Maestro lifts his hands
And ghosts of young men, tall and proud, go marching through the glen
While strains of all the "rebel" songs of Ireland echo clearly
And with each generation,these songs are heard again

Oh, varied are your melodies, O lovely Connemara
Along your wild mountain paths, your rough and tumbling seas
But in your restless beauty, all the plaintive music lingers
And carries Connemara's song on every gentle breeze

COUNTY MAYO

There's a tiny bit of Paradise
With a special heav'nly glow
Nestled in the west of Ireland
The County of Mayo

The birthplace of my forebears
My roots are solid there
And other counties, other towns
Just never can compare

Ballyhaunis and Claremorris
And Clare Island on the bay
There couldn't be a nicer place
To spend a holiday

The rolling hills and fields abound
With forty shades of green
The moonlight shining on Clew Bay
Is the loveliest e'er seen

The sweetly blooming heather
The rhodedendrons fair
And lovely old stone fences
Dot the landscape everywhere

The beautiful old landmarks
We saw throughout Mayo
The old "round towers," Clare Island's Cliffs
The sheer, sheer drop below

The old and crumbling castles
So often told in song
And then that beauteous wonder
Ashford Castle down in Cong

But the people of the County
Therein its treasure lies
They have to be the friendliest
'Neath Erin's sunny skies

They just can't do enough to make
The stranger feel at ease
No matter what your needs are
They are always there to please

No, that's one place I will ne'er forget
Wherever I may go
Its memory is with me yet
The County of Mayo

HAIKU

Japanese Poetry Form

WINTER'S NIGHT TAPESTRY

Starlight through the trees
Forms delicate filigree
On the soft white snow

VIEW FROM A PLANE

Snow-capped mountains rise
Majestic in their shadows
Yet seem very small

EMPTY CHURCH

Candles flicker low
Shadows fall on empty pews
Is God forgotten?

THUNDERSTORM

Across threatening skies
Race fierce black clouds in anger
Crying bitter tears

THE TIGHT ROPE WALKER

High above the crowds
She glides across the thin wire
Grace personified

IS IT SPRING YET ??

The tiny green shoots
Look perplexed wearing snow caps
On their newborn heads

POTTER'S FIELD

A little white cross
Planted deep in the hillside
Somber sentinel

HUNGER

Ethiopia
Small children with large, sad eyes
Tear at the heart strings

BY ANY OTHER NAME

A single red rose
Made perfect by God's own hand
Heavenly sculpture

HOLOCAUST

In silent terror
They wait as the marching feet
Come closer, then halt!

AFTER THE RAIN

The crystal clear sky
Swept clean by the summer storm
Glistens in sunlight

MORNING IN SCOTLAND

Opalescent mist
Covers the low hills and lochs
In gauzy splendor

IRELAND

Soft, refreshing mist
Rolling hills of verdant green
Ireland in the spring

JUST AFTER DAWN

Morning clouds linger
Forming gossamer shadows
O'er the wak'ning hills

IN COOL REPOSE

In blankets of snow
Their lacy arms extended
The winter trees sleep

IT'S SPRING!

A chirping robin
Hops about in happy song
Heralding the spring

NESTLINGS

Tiny beaks protrude
From the tightly woven nest
Waiting for breakfast

THE UNKNOWN SOLDIER

The wind blows gently
And stirs the crimson poppies
O'er his nameless grave

TIDE'S OUT

In the cool, moist sand
Resting on their small elbows
The patient boats wait

SOLACE

In your darkest hour
When you know you can't go on
Take heart - God loves you!

AUTUMN

Scent of burning leaves
Fiery reds and golds explode
Into Autumn days

TANKA

Japanese Poetry Form

FLIGHT OF THE DOVE

In tranquil beauty
The dove flies across the sky
A ripple of white
Its wings curling in the sun
A silken ribbon of flight

DAWN

Reach for the new dawn
As the rose climbs to the sun
As the tiny child
Raises trusting arms for love
For in each dawn there is hope

SUMMER SONG

White marshmallow clouds
Play hide-and-seek with bluebirds
Through summer breezes
Dainty flowers nod and wave
At bright butterflies in flight

SUMMER'S LEGACY

Summer's legacy
Gentle winds that shake the corn
And sway the daisies
Butterflies that flutter by
And the kiss of a warm sun

ALOHA

Tradewinds softly blow
Dark-eyed boys with steel guitars
Strum their melodies
Flowered leis and sun-drenched smiles
Say welcome to Hawaii!

RUFFLES

Pom pons and ruffles
A wide smile belying his
Aching heart inside
The sad little clown tumbles
Making all the children laugh

FOURTH OF JULY PARADE

Rap-tap-tapping drums
Trumpets blast and children sing
Marching down the street
Waving flags as we salute
The birthday of our nation

HALLOWEEN

In the dark stillness
A night bird screeches, it's cry
Awakening spirits
Who lurk behind old gnarled trees
And dance among the shadows

BONNY SCOTLAND

White clouds floating by
Strains of bagpipes fill the air
Across moor and glen
Fields of fragrant heather bring
Autumn to bonny Scotland

KENNEDY

A bright light still shines
For this man loved by many
An eternal flame
And still crowds of mourners come
To silently stand and pray

AUTUMN IN MAINE

Bright golden colors
Scalloped with deep crimson hues
Say "Welcome to Maine"
While quaint little antique shops
Beckon shyly to strangers

"HIS MESSAGE"

Once in a season
As brilliant light rays are formed
By the setting sun
One can almost hear God say
"This is My Son - Hear ye Him!"

IMAGE

Stand tall and be proud
For you are a child of God
Made in His image
Let no man deny your right
To attain your highest goals

MY ROSE GARDEN

The warmth of the sun
Sparkles the dew on the leaves
Caressed by the breeze
And kisses each tiny bud
To fulfill its promised bloom

OLD WARRIORS ON THE WHARF

Charcoal silhouettes
Tall ships bowing and weaving
In the evening breeze
Play a sunset symphony
As they creak inside their bones

AUTUMN BALLET

Crisp dried leaves skitter
As if dancing on their toes
Across the pavement
Twirling like ballerinas
Choreographed by the winds

COLD'N MOMENTS

Lacy silhouettes
Stand against late Autumn skies
Majestic barren trees
Keeping their lonely vigil
As cold winter rushes in

WINTER'S ROYALTY

Stately autumn trees
Shake loose their vibrant colors
Of crimson and gold
Then raise their barren branches
To be clothed in white velvet

OUR WEDDING BELLE

She walks down the aisle
A vision in lace and net
And smiling sweetly
She squeezes her father's arm
While I watch through happy tears

THINK GREEN

On my window sill
A pot of bright green shamrocks
With small white blossoms
Reminding me of fun days
Wandering Ireland's meadows

ABOUT THE AUTHOR

Marian Grady McNeely, mother of five, grandmother of ten was born and raised in Chicago, Illinois. She attended DePaul University, majoring in English and is a member of the Chicago-based Poets and Patrons, Inc.

Marian has won many creative writing awards in contests sponsored by Poets and Patrons and the Illinois Federation of Women's Clubs. Four of her poems have represented the state of Illinois at the General Federation of Women's Club's competitions throughout the United States. She has also been published in many newspapers and magazines in the Chicago area and in several periodicals in Ireland.

She currently resides in Palatine, Illinois with her husband, Walter.